Table of Contents

So you are young, single, and attractive and no doubt have many eligible men pursuing you. Be ready to cut my head off but I truly believe the problem with most these men is that if they aren't already married, there is probably something wrong with them. Experts claim that there are so many perfectly eligible single guys out there but have they dated any of these men they are piling into the eligible pool? Here are some problems my "total package" friends and I have come across:

- **No manners** (blatant stuff you just can't ignore…. taking calls during your date, etc…)

- **Insensitive** (my ex is crazy, you don't mind if I drink 5 beers at lunch, right?)
- **Baggage** (I'm going through a custody battle right now, I have to live with my parents for the time being, it's only temporary)

- **Chauvinism** (You're not voting for Hillary, right? You're not one of those kind of women that... etc....)
- **Egotism** (Calling you all the time like YOU have nothing better to do than jump every time they call & GOD FORBID you may be smart and dating others!)
- **Unavailable** (I'm just waiting for the right person, I don't believe in marriage or won't do it again, I like to keep my options open, I'm a workaholic, etc...)
- **Casanova** (I'm never attracted to anyone else when I'm in a relationship, you're so gorgeous it hurts, ...I never cheat, do you? My last girlfriend did drugs, cheated, and used me...)

- **Desperate** (they barely know you but know they want to be with you...I mean, you're great & you know it but the feeling you could probably have a ring on your finger in a month doesn't make you feel too special, does it?)
- **Selfish** (talk most of the time, not really too concerned with your beliefs, your goals, your job, etc.... these types assume whatever you think now will be converted later)

Sound familiar? After exhausting your time and energy treading water in that eligibility pool you begin to wonder if your standards are too high or if you've watched too many romance movies. You talk to your other friends and laugh about how you could write a book about all your common dating experiences and may even come to the conclusion that all these guys are just "immature" or maybe even older men are the answer.

[When you start to brainstorm at this level and in this situation, something important is happening in your thought process: You are more comfortable defining what you don't want than what you do want. It is easier. It is much harder to think about the kind of person you will have to become in order to attract the type of man you want. So instead, you allow the behaviors of the men you've been dating to take front seat so you can free yourself of the responsibility of exploring the unknown* which is how you need to improve yourself. It is much safer to explore what you know you don't want because what you don't want is what's 'not good enough', not yourself. This self-imposed limitation is the equivalent to "treading water" because your focus is more on **what** you are attracting now/or will attract than **how** you can attract what you want in the future. This leaves you very vulnerable, especially to all variations of unavailable men].

You then find yourself at that point where you have no real motivation to continue treading water in the same pool and need different results because you still have that glimmer of hope that what those experts say is true. Having that "glimmer of hope" is a seductive trap where you go from playing an active role in determining your future to a passive one; it is not optimism in light of your past experiences. It is a limit so what you will attract will be limited because you expect something different from continually redefining what you won't tolerate. This is where a lot of women wonder, "How will I **recognize** the right person?" instead of becoming the right person. But let's keep it light because all that is uninteresting.

Are you now cynical, bored, suspicious, and somewhat defeated? Are you relieved to find out others are going through the same thing you are and get energy sharing the drama? Do you find confidence in the fact you would never tolerate a lot of what goes on in marriages today and what these women put up with? Are you too picky? Your married friends might think so but more importantly, what you really are is **ripe pickings** for a married man. Whoa! How did we get there so fast? Have you ever heard the phrases **"I don't know how this all happened"** or **"It all just happened so fast!"** typically be followed by "to me"? You are way too independent for that!

Don't believe me? Here is what is in the works already: A married man who has become routine in his duties as a father, husband, and provider at some point decides he wants a little sexual excitement and his ego fed. He has felt this way for a while but instead of exploring what it will take to prevent him from acting on this, he tells himself it is normal or a phase in his marriage. He also believes that if his wife understood him better or admired/boosted his ego more, he wouldn't feel this way. He will never communicate that because it will require him to adjust his reality and be more responsible for his ego.

[It is not always a communication problem or a loss of interest in his wife that triggers this; it is a flaw in the message he keeps confirming to himself that serves his purpose and gives him permission to act when the situation arises. Have you ever heard men say, "It's okay to be attracted to someone as long as I don't act on it"? This rids them of all responsibility of developing a relationship with a woman they are attracted to so long as they don't physically make a move. They benefit from this, just like a single unavailable man, because it allows them to feed off female attention with no obligation. Statistics show that it is the woman that controls, through verbal and non-verbal cues, and sets the pace in a romantic relationship and it is the man who responds. They don't have to do much but sit back and enjoy the show. As long as the married man believes the logic he is feeding himself and receives a gain from it, his vulnerability will keep surfacing no matter how good the marriage is. He will say "I don't know how this happened!" or "It was just an accident!" to protect his future ego feed supply].

If you are getting angry with me, good, keep reading!

However the two of you come across one another, it is almost going to feel like an instant attraction and a mutual recognition of **"understanding each other"**. This typically happens in an office setting or through other

work-related activities where there is the
opportunity and the setting to subtly exchange
non-verbal cues, which will lead to this attraction.
Is this feeling real? Yes, and it's intense!
Would you feel this way if he weren't married
and appropriate for you? NO! (I'll explain later)
The script unfolds predictably where you become
a **special friend** and the two of you have
harmless lunches, coffee, etc… At this point you
may be asking your friends what they think
because nothing physical has happened. It's really
simple. This is stage one of the seduction process.
How are you seducing one another?
He listens to every word you say, is a gentleman,
pays for everything, considers your feelings,
believes in you and your goals, compliments you,
loves that your smart and feisty, wants you to talk
about yourself, seems in awe that you are
spending time with him, and respects your time
and what you have to say. In other words, here is

a man that seems to **RECOGNIZE YOUR WORTH.**

You are in awe of him for his dedication to his career accomplishments, his kids, and maybe even his wife. You respect him for the sacrifices he has made and you really listen to him and express your admiration. You are probably even more open and flirtatious with this man because it has a great affect on him and he doesn't react with desperation/eagerness. For him, here is a woman that **FEEDS HIS EGO** and is **SEXUALLY STIMULATING**.

[He is also keeping his new "friendship" from his wife a secret but what he tells himself is that it's the attraction to you that is the secret. This rationalization allows him to continue his behavior and remove any responsibility he has in developing a relationship with you. It also allows him to keep you "compartmentalized" as an attraction rather than as a person; he is more excited by the interest you reflect back at him than the excitement that comes from getting to know you. This compartmentalization will be a constant throughout the affair or it would be impossible for him to maintain his marriage and his affair with you].

This is when the stage is set for an affair

You can't deny that the physical tension is building and your desire to become closer to this person is very strong. You feel very empowered by the effect you have on him like you have a life raft with his name on it and you could throw it out to him or pull it back at will (he is willing to risk everything for you). And this man isn't going to just spend his time or be attracted to anyone. He is discriminating.

I'm going to interrupt this chemistry-induced soul-mate experience and explain some basic concepts:

We have already established how each of you was **vulnerable** to each other in the first place. You were treading water in a pool of emotionally crippled men and to keep from stagnating, you stuck to your standards and refused to settle. You are a strong woman and are determined to face reality and have come to the realization that **reality ain't so pretty**. And, no, there is nothing wrong/unrealistic/cynical with you or your view on things but this will change. Part of the reason you are able to indulge in this attraction is because you believe there is something missing in his marriage and that for him to develop this relationship with you means he finds you too alluring to resist. Simple... right?

He was treading water in his daily routine and probably came to acknowledge or even resolved himself to the fact that this was probably the best it was going to get. I'm giving this guy (because he is an exception, right?) the benefit of the doubt. However, it is far more likely his routine includes dipping into the pool of attractive, smart, single women like you who are more emotionally mature and won't settle for those cripples. This is important because in that specific pool he is dipping into are women that will **RECOGNIZE HIS VALUE**. Unlike a weaker, more needy woman, an emotionally sophisticated, independent woman like you will appreciate the gentleman that he is.

The other remaining pools of women are either too old, married (limited time/energy) ......or emotionally immature (single, very young, possibly more attractive, fickle, unreliable) and cannot give him the required emotional, intellectual, and physical energy that you will soon be providing.

His beliefs, views, feelings (unlike yours) on life will not be changing but you are not aware of this yet because you're too busy feeling empowered right now.

What's the worse that can happen? You feel great with that life raft in your hand and you can always date other people! You deserve consistent sex by someone who cares/loves you and who knows, maybe the right person will pop up during this whole experience and you can kind of exit the whole scene with your predetermined script that goes something like this: "I just can't do this anymore, you're married and this was bound to happen…we both knew I would have so many options and it's time now for me to explore those…. you know I love you but it's time for me to go". You dramatically make your exit and he is devastated. You prance off with your new love and either trash that symbolic life raft or tuck it away for safekeeping. You probably envision the latter since giving up power is very unappealing. You have nothing to lose and he is risking everything. This may or may not even be about love for you.

Am I trying to make you sound capricious and evil? No, and you're not. If you can admit that you have fantasized these things, you are ready to see that this is a crucial step in the seduction process and it is called **Losing Your Sense of Reality.** For those women who cannot admit this and want to firmly stand by their innocence (it just happened! Our love is profound & and an exception) in the seduction process, are going to be the ones that fall the hardest. They may never get out. If this is you, stop reading now because this writer is not at all interested in contributing to your defense of an exceptional love experience.

If this man was your true love growing up and you really know him better than his wife and just happened to be separated by tragic circumstances, this article is not for you and you probably wouldn't feel compelled to read it in the first place. He would be divorced, remarried to you and you would be way too busy planning your new life.

We will now continue and as you can see, some of us will be weeded out along the way. If you've read this far and opt out later, take heart, you will have already instilled in yourself an important reality benchmark that you will come back to later and I hope you save this article for when you are ready to absorb it.

Remember, your strength so far has kept you from marrying an idiot or gave you the courage to divorce one, has kept you on the pursuit of reality (up until now), and has built the foundation for a magnetic, sensual, capable, intellectual woman who radiates these qualities with confidence.

You may not trust your competence in relationships (we all question that, even your married friends) and may feel some guilt about your relationship or the secrets you are now carrying and worry if the weight of those things are going to impact your self esteem or ruin your reputation because of this situation. Not really. If you felt too guilty and had a problem hiding things, you wouldn't be in this situation and that is why it is so easy to move forward in it because these aren't the battles you will be fighting. Are you a bad person because of this? No, this is just another step in **losing your reality** and it is an important one because once you feel you can conquer what you perceive to be the true obstacles, you are confident to move forward. For women, this disillusioned thought process usually marks the beginning of the physical affair although it can happen after but regardless, it does happen. For the married man, your emotional process (the planning of how the affair will work, what it means, how often you will see each other) is very important because your anticipation and excitement about the new relationship will allow him to qualify you in a way that would have seemed too intrusive before: "You're not an angry/revengeful person, are you?" or other questions that you shouldn't have to defend or explain. You may even find yourself making sure he covers his tracks or not asking certain questions for fear he'll think you're the "fatal attraction type". What is actually a negotiation process will look like natural concerns/reassurances anyone would have and need if they were risking their marriage and family to be with you.

[How the negotiation process works: A married man will often tell you that he had no idea this would lead to an affair and what started out as an innocent friendship resulted in an overwhelming attraction to you. He may even admit how attracted to you he was initially but never thought he would act on it. He may even tell you this is the first time he has ever cheated on his wife. There are many variations of this but it will all boil down to one thing: it was who you were, how gorgeous you were, how "whatever" you were that made him willing/tempted/powerless to disrupt his everyday life and take a risk to be with you. **You have just lost round one.** You have just taken full responsibility for the development of this affair. You may know full well his role in it (you may know he knows you know and may think it's cute) but that won't matter from here on out (even if he admits it later). The person that accepts the responsibility for something is the person who will invest more into that something. For him to be responsible for the pursuit of this relationship would mean that he was no longer functioning in the same compartmentalized manner and was created something apart from that. It also establishes you as the initiator and that provides him a built in exit strategy; he fails to meet your requests and you get angry so he can tell you how bad he feels that he can't give you more and then withdraws in defeat.

What you have told him by your actions is that it is okay for you to be in a relationship where you take 100% responsibility for your needs and feelings and when your needs aren't met, it is because you are asking for too much. His anxiety is also greatly reduced by this. From his perspective, he isn't risking anything more than what he had been except that the secret compartment (the generalized attractions he feels that he keeps separate from his wife) is going to be activated into relationship form. Your relationship will be contained within that compartment (say 10% of his life) so his emotional involvement in his marriage will not decrease].

*For woman who are **CURRENTLY**, not intending or planning, dating two or more* *married men, this does not apply to you and you should stop reading.*

You may not believe or understand how this works but it does and has repeatedly with success, usually at a subconscious level so he is probably not evil. And no, he is not out to get you or maliciously planning all this. Earlier we discussed how he was not desperate or overly eager (if he was, you would have been disgusted like you were with the single guys) and that is part of the reason why; if he were not interested in securing your emotional involvement, he would have dipped in another pool. He is also very familiar with how he has compartmentalized his life so you are not a new addition but a replacement (his generalized attractions now have a focus). This is not a pretty dynamic, is it? Once you are emotionally and physically involved in this relationship, you will feel a subtle shift on your empowerment scale even though you may not recognize it as that. This feeling usually surfaces after the excitement of the relationship starts to plateau. You will attribute this shift to a struggle within yourself about the false battles you are having with guilt and secrecy or maybe even ask yourself if you are limiting your options by seeing this man. This still may or may not be about love for you and you may smirk at the idea that you are emotionally involved. If you are in denial about being emotionally involved at this point, you need to keep reading and face reality: If you met this married man on a cruise or in a bar and had a brief physical relationship and now it's over, you wouldn't still be reading this or compelled to read it in the first place.

What is really happening is you fear you are losing your grip on that life raft; it's like he's getting too comfortable with the risks he's taking. He is not taking it from you and he may even be spending more time with you and will probably remain just as attentive as ever because **married men will work harder than single men at trying to make you fall for them**. His behavior is actually not changing at all but you are now struggling to understand why you don't feel as empowered as you did and it has nothing to do with him although you will eventually project* it on to him. It may frustrate you that as the relationship becomes more involved and intense and obviously mutual, he is still just as compartmentalized. It just doesn't seem natural and maybe you have overlooked something important. You start analyzing the relationship up to this point and going over everything you can remember. You begin treading water.

Here are the signs when you have reached this stage:

You may want to make him feel a little jealous

- You may wonder about his sex life with his wife

- You may notice you are no longer interested in other guys (if you haven't dated anyone recently this applies to you)

- You may want him to fall in love with you

- You may get upset if he doesn't call you when you need support

- You would love to be a fly on the wall at times when you are not with him

- You don't think he will ever lie to you (you completely trust him) or you wonder if he has or will ever lie to you

Is this just normal curiosity? NO, not at this
stage because you are searching for reasons why
you don't feel as good and you're looking to him.
This is the danger zone for you and you may or
may not want to acknowledge that and chances
are, you will dismiss it as curiosity or being upset
over nothing. Getting caught up in whether you
are just harmlessly curious isn't really
important because what's not up for debate is one
simple fact: If you admit you are wondering
these things, you are spending more and more
energy on this relationship. You see, guilt and
secrecy is not the true enemy but the **energy you
expend is**. This still has nothing to do with him
because the rules haven't changed and he hasn't
changed but you are changing although you may
or may not be in love (the love thing actually isn't
that important and you will see why later). What
you are experiencing is a gradual loss of that
surge of power you felt at the beginning and you

want that feeling back so you will project this outside yourself onto him in the form of a power struggle within the actual relationship. You will comfort your ego by fantasizing about those times you had the most effect on him, the beginning stages and then blame him for not providing this to you.

The **green light** for the next round of negotiation signals when you are convinced he has the upper hand; this is the transition where you realize you don't hold his life raft at all. Remember, he has not taken it from you but at this point (you lost it in the negotiation process), he will start to lie to you in response to your insecurities and you will be treading water at a faster pace just to stay sane. Here are some of the signs you are at this stage:

- You think it's odd that you can have such a great time together but he can go back home and be normal

- You feel the greatest progression in the relationship was in the beginning, even though he knows you more now

- You think it's strange that he could just go on like this forever and be fine with it

- You think he's cruel to his wife to do this to her and can't believe she hasn't caught on

- You start thinking about getting out but it just feels too overwhelming to make that decision right now

- You have a close relationship with him but it's not very satisfying

- You have to create drama just to get him to respond to you in a way that you don't feel taken for granted

- You would definitely discourage/warn a friend from getting into something like this

- You think he probably lies about how boring his life is to spare your feelings

It is time to weed out some people who will not get any benefit from reading any further.
If you truly believe you want this man to leave his wife and family and start over with you and think it will work, STOP reading and please see a therapist with or without him before you do a lot of damage. If you just have those thoughts/fantasies sometimes and have not acted on them or if that thought horrifies you, please

continue to read this because I think it may help you.

What you have lost in this round is your special friendship. Once he feels you are starting to hold him responsible for your feelings, your value to him begins to decline. Ironically, this is when women usually start to project this onto the wife "I feel so bad for her, if she only knew, how can she be so unaware?". Her value is starting to increase even though you take comfort in thinking that at least you're not her.

We will assume the best case scenario from here on out and assume this married man continues to treat you well, pay attention to you, tell you or not tell you he loves you, confide in you about his wife or not, etc....

These things seem very important so you are probably hyper alert to any fluctuating behavior on his part, but right now you are most disturbed with the whole idea of him lying to spare your feelings. Why would he need to do that? What if he is lying about other things? What was so great about our relationship was that we wouldn't have to lie to one another! Just as experts claim how many eligible single men are out there, they also claim that any man that lies to his wife will eventually lie to you. In fact, they adamantly assert the whole foundation of this type of relationship is based on a lie. Frankly, I am amazed at the ability to lump everyone into these categories as if we all follow some predictable pattern. Women get really caught up in this and I believe it actually contributes to women staying in these relationships longer even though that's not the intent of these professionals. Why? We identified **energy expended** as enemy number one and the amount of energy you are expending in this relationship is proportionate to how invested you are in it; therefore, it becomes an excellent indicator of how long you will stay. Let's put this whole lying thing into the right context so you're not subjecting yourself to this nonsense and entertaining suspicions of being the latest victim of a most sophisticated manipulator:

- You knew going in that he was willing to lie to his wife and you were okay with that (you moving forward was your consent- you can't back out of that one now!)

- You **trusted** him enough to know he was not going to purposely sabotage you or your reputation (you are strong and you don't put up with evil, emotional cripples)

- You also knew that you **trusted** him to be sensitive enough to your feelings that you felt confident starting this relationship

🌾 You admired the fact he was stable and responsible in his life and **trusted** he wouldn't do anything crazy and impulsive to harm anyone; in other words, a pretty decent guy

🌾 You **trusted** him enough to give yourself physically and emotionally to him without a commitment because he fulfilled a genuine need of yours & vice versa

🌾 You **trusted** that he sincerely wanted to make you happy given his serious restraints of time and energy

Your gut feelings were right! You could and you still can trust him with these things because you are strong and smart enough to rely on those seasoned instincts of yours. He hasn't changed these qualities about himself and probably won't so don't worry and question yourself to death about it. The truth is, your gut feelings and intuition are still working at this point so please don't waste your energy chipping away at the great qualities you possess and will need later. So then why did I bring up the whole lying thing just like the experts continually do? Why does this strike a cord in so many women in these situations? The answer to that has to do with our perception that there exists an enemy outside of us, beyond our control, and that feels very threatening. With our life raft given away and the power within the relationship being more balanced (if it weren't and you still had all that power via the symbolic life raft, you'd be bored and have moved on already), the reality that the relationship is capped in it's potential starts to sink in. A successful relationship is one that continually grows so any perceived outside threat is diminished in its capacity to destroy because this relationship's uncapped growth can offset it. The outside threat you see is that you got into a situation based on the picture he presented to you and now you question how forthright he was. You get angry because you feel like he is getting away with a lot and doesn't seem to be too concerned about what you have had to sacrifice. As he's planning his next family vacation, you start to fantasize about meeting the love of your life, creating unexplained absences, having your own mysterious double life, etc. Until thoughts like "maybe he's interested in someone else", or "maybe he is getting bored" interrupt your daydreaming.

If you are not bothered by this whole lying thing/painting false picture or even disturbed by the possibility of him seeing someone else (no, not his wife) in addition to you, you probably don't need to read any more.

Your questioning has more to do with doubting your reasonable and rightful expectation to grow and explore life to its fullest than it has to do with him. If there is any doubt in your mind that this may not be the case, remember that you have made tremendous strides by not settling in that stagnant pool of immature and selfish men that most women will end up marrying. If women didn't continue to have sex and marry these men, there wouldn't be so many of them. But let's get back to business.

Thus far, in your relationship with this married man, you have invested a healthy amount of energy (whether you love him or not) and I'm glad we can finally agree on that. Unlike what is happening now, the prior energy required to date those losers left you feeling defeated but it didn't really demand an "emotional investment"; you were able to throw that out and pull it back at will and even on your own time. Why am I reminding you of this? Because...

What you are still failing to really internalize, which was what got you into this married man thing in the first place, is the pure fact that **reality isn't so pretty**. That's a hard one to swallow because **it's true,** so keep reading because once you get past that, it won't appear as imminent and threatening as it does now. I promise. You just don't understand what it really means yet and it does sound like the worst kind of enemy to face. Why explore life to it's fullest when most likely things can only get worse? If you didn't believe this, you would stop investing more into your current relationship that is making you feel bad and invest more into your future.

When you fail to admit that you have a right to expect growth in yourself and that reality is difficult, you will begin to believe your married man isn't doing enough. You will believe he is lying or manipulating you, that you can't get out, that he is keeping you from a good life, that you are angry with him because you spend holidays alone, etc…

This is your signal that you are investing an increasing amount of negative energy into an already limited relationship because you would rather see it die a slow death than take the action required to leave it with some self-respect. He hasn't changed and he hasn't changed the rules of the relationship on you. What you will start to do more of is projecting expectations onto him (that you know he can't fulfill) so you don't have to face what you need to in order to keep on that path of growing because it is too scary. Can you guess what those expectations have to do with? You got it! **Safety and Security**. Once again, this has nothing to do with him but this has everything to do with your fear of not being able to provide these things for yourself, even though that's what you're already doing for yourself despite him. You are not weak and passive; it is natural to resist what it takes to grow sometimes.

You just don't realize how much he is not giving you.

He stopped growing a long time ago. At some point, he realized the same thing you did and decided not to face reality at all, in his own self and in his marriage. He is comfortable with this and does not want to change it or else he would have already. The pain of this relationship and the longing/need you have for each other is actually coming from very different places: You are a strong, vibrant woman with passion and strong feelings who is just afraid right now having growing pains and he feels pain about not being able to make you happy (how he makes you feel boosts his ego). He's not dumb and he does care about you and your feelings so don't spend a lot of energy thinking he's selfish and a taker. He wants to meet your needs like he did with so much ease in the beginning but he is incapable so he will lie in order to get back those good feelings and to keep you just like he lies to his wife in order to maintain the marriage and keep her. Is this reality pretty? To you, it is prettier than the "unknown" reality you were previously facing or else you would have already left the relationship. Back to your married man: He almost sounds pathetic in that context and how could someone you admired so much be that pathetic? He's not: he still remains all of those things you admired but has made different choices for his life that won't change because he is comfortable with them. You are the one that is no longer comfortable. Best case scenario is that when you get out of this he will just let you go but most of the time the married man will start promising things in order to keep you and maintain his level of comfort. What this should tell you is that the lies/promises he makes are in direct proportion to how resistant he really is to change. You are forcing change on him when it is you that wants to grow. When a person lies to you to soothe your emotions, they are not investing in your emotional growth; they are trying to avoid it.

This is the stage most of the experts focus on because this is where extramarital affairs usually progress and stay stuck the longest. By the way, there is no progression from this stage because it's the last one. It's not going anywhere and this is the best it's going to get if you want to call this good. This is where the energy you expend on your expectations of him is proportionate to the damage you are going to do to yourself; meaning, you have stopped treading water and you are beginning to go under. This is where the weaker women get crazy and lose it; but he chose you because you are strong. If this sounds confusing it is because what the experts have drilled into your subconscious doesn't make sense:

Being with a married man is a waste of your time

Falling in love with a married man will break
your heart

He will never leave his wife

He will lie to you and you will be waiting forever

Notice how the above statements have absolutely
nothing to do with what you have been reading?
If you took serious issue with the above
statements, you would have never entered this
arrangement in the first place, despite how
tempting it is to claim those statements now (just
like when you wanted so bad to belief your true
battles were going to be secrecy and guilt). This
is where society further contributes to your **loss
of reality**.

Those statements imply you are in a passive state
just waiting to be given the time, energy, and love
you deserve when actually it's the opposite. You
are the one actively expending a vast amount of
emotionally energy while the married man is in a
passive state. Simply put, he is not wasting your

time but rather, you are actively pursuing your own stagnation and with a passion. Falling in love with him isn't the real danger here because falling in love is a temporary, passive state, which requires very little energy on your part. Remember how easy it was for him to make you feel good in the beginning by just being there? It was almost as if it didn't require any effort on his part. Amazing! That statement is not only misleading but it contributes to your **loss of reality** by insinuating your love will destroy you when love isn't the issue here (whether you love him or not). Love is an act; a choice to contribute to the growth of another human being despite whatever mood or expectation one has at any given moment. If you have gotten this far, you probably have done those things for him but that is not what you are in pain about. You are not in pain due to a love dilemma. You are in pain because this situation did not alter the reality you tried to escape and you are mourning the disillusioned self; attempting to hold on to your innocent self (the self that thought reality was pretty). It brought you right back to the same issue to work through again except you added another person. Predictably, you have projected this onto a married man because it feels safer. If facing reality felt safer you wouldn't be in this situation.

He will never leave his wife doesn't address why you don't leave either because that would require energy from him and then you would be required to stop your active pursuit of stagnation and you are not ready to do that. As long as you are expending energy treading that water, you can avoid what you didn't want to face initially. You just don't know what you want.

This has nothing to do with him because he hasn't changed. If you fail to grasp what is going on in this last stage of the relationship, you will either remain here for years until he ends it with you or you will become so tired you will not be able to feed him what he needs to stay comfortable. He may love you or not love you, which will have nothing to do with the reason it ends, but it will feel that way. You may feel like a fool and kick yourself for not listening to what has been said about dating married men but if you truly understand the dynamic, you will avoid all this nonsense and go through the suffering in a way that is honest and constructive.

Back to the part where you start to drown: The energy you don't realize your spending is starting to feel horrible and therefore you believe the relationship is always going to be unbalanced in his favor. To compensate for this imbalance, you start getting angry and making requests of him you never pictured doing. His failure at giving you what you perceive you need makes you feel even more inadequate, which he senses and doesn't like, so he in turn compensates by telling you or promising you things to alleviate your pain. He is not an evil liar and he may even be making those promises or saying those things because he loves you and can't stand to see you in pain. Have you ever heard the phrase "love is not enough"? It's true in any relationship or marriage so it does apply to your special situation. His lies and promises may make you feel better temporarily because it seems like you are receiving something you need. You have been furiously treading water for a while now so it is normal for you to be on the lookout for a life raft. You are on survival mode and what will drown you is your failure to correctly identify **enemy** and **rescuer**. Where you once questioned your competency in relationships. You will now betray your instincts.

When people speak of the "**other woman**" settling for the crumbs of a married man and how desperate she must in fact be, are the supposed experts who perpetuate a false reality, because if this were true, she would have married a man from that first pool of emotional cripples. It is overactive attempts to avoid the pain of facing reality that is causing her pain, exhaustion, and heartache. Not this married man, this relationship, or this waiting. These crumbs he is supposedly tossing her are not symbolic of his leftover love or his leftover emotional involvement or his leftover extra energy he is tossing her in this crisis. They are the opposite. He hasn't changed and he doesn't want to change because he is comfortable. For him to expend any more energy in any particular direction at all doesn't make sense because it would cause him discomfort and discomfort prompts people to change. Therefore, whatever crumbs he is throwing her are not an attempt to increase his emotional investment but an attempt to now avoid it. The lies and promises are designed to replace the energy he was initially giving and she accepts it even though what she is receiving is less. Both of them falsely believe they are actually contributing more to the relationship while getting less out of it. Society is backing this woman's belief that his crumbs represent love and emotional investment (energy) which will lead her to conclude that the potential emptiness of his promises are the **enemy** and he is her **rescuer**. He is holding the life raft with her name on it and why he refuses to give it to her will paint him as a worthless liar and her as a pathetic, passive person waiting for the love she will never get.

The situation itself then becomes her higher power even though he's not holding her life raft now just as she wasn't holding his in the beginning. There was never any life raft because she grossly miscalculated what he was risking for her. His only risk was in whom he selected and he chose well; she would turn on herself before she lashed out at him. Ok, even if the life raft existed symbolically in this scenario, it was still incorrectly representing "power over a person". A more accurate representation would be "projection" so it would be impossible for someone else to hold your life raft. Since she felt powerless over her situation, she was seduced by the perception she had power over someone else. He did not seduce her. Life raft is a pretty dramatic description of the whole dynamic and another blatant misrepresentation of what was really going on; safety raft fits better. She felt safe when she believed he was risking everything and under these circumstances alone, she felt empowered enough to move forward in a relationship with limited potential.

You may have not noticed that the discussion stopped focusing on you in a direct manner and shifted to discussing you like a statistic or a category you were lumped into like you were on some sort of backburner. You may feel taken for granted, lied to, and treated like a dumping ground for false promises; provided you are still under the belief that your married man actually would expend that much time and energy to get those kind of results. **Does that make you angry?** Why? You are the one that changed the rules and destroyed a perfectly comfortable relationship with your misplaced expectations. You are the one that thought you could bypass all the hard work it takes to earn and build a real relationship and simply have that love miraculously projected onto you. You created this whole life raft concept to fill yourself with power and confidence only to use it against yourself and him later. Not only did he never participate in the whole life raft scenario, **he never knew it existed**. He never gave up anything.

Do you remember in the beginning when you felt great and had those fantasies about how you would end things and how devastated he would be? You wouldn't have believed me if I told you earlier but maybe you are ready to hear it now. He is not so pathetic that his lies and comfort zone will cause him doom in the end although it's comforting for you to believe that. He was actually spending the same amount of energy you were but it was on his family. By working, doing yard work, having dinners at home, spending weekends with his wife and kids, he was consistently showing you through his actions where his love was being exercised. Remember, love is an action. You may discount this and believe anyone who lies and cheats can't possibly be happy but what good would it do to side with the experts? If they (your married man and his wife) were uncomfortable, they would change it. He never tried to determine what would make you happy or try to change you. He accepted you the way you were either because he thought you were amazing, or because it would have required more of his energy not to.

He was not capable of feeling the intensity of emotion towards you or share in your pain throughout this experience because 90% of his energy was going towards maintaining and probably even improving what he already had. How can this person feel devastated? I guess he could feel 10% devastated.

Before you start feeling like the most low impact person alive, you need to realize this isn't **personal** and I can almost guarantee the last thing he wanted to do was hurt you. Was he acting in your best interests or really respecting your feelings? No, but he doesn't even give that to his wife and she was the one he married and had kids with. Comparing yourself in any way to his family is absolutely ridiculous because if love from a guy like that was what you wanted, you would already be married to a guy like him. Was it a lie that he was super into you and felt a rush of adrenaline being around you? No, but that wasn't **personal** either. That was his projection but his projections didn't go any farther than that. Remember, all he was looking for was some stimulation. You were looking for your **worth** to be defined by something or someone other than yourself. You also negotiated all of your worth in the beginning of the relationship.

That dating pool you got out of before you met him consisted of guys like him. He was probably a combination of what you wouldn't expect: The egotist mixed with a little emotional unavailability and maybe some over eagerness in the beginning to secure the attachment of his wife. You have already graduated from that pool of emotional cripples and the only reason you didn't spot him was because his primary feeding was already being taken care of enough at home to allow the appearance of a more balanced man. Are you that needy even though you've been statistically placed in the needy and desperate group? Lets see, you spent 10% of your time in a relationship that offered no commitment and you didn't date other people. Even though 90% of your time was spent on a furious race towards stagnation and is considered self-destructive, you do keep yourself pretty well entertained! I mean, that 90% relationship you had with yourself and your inner demons was pretty intense!

You're just pissed at him because he didn't turn on himself like you did but you realize you're only projecting again so you don't act out on that now. You know that you are just angry because growing up requires you to look after your own best interests and you don't want to have to do that! But you will because you are strong and you want to grow. Unlike a child, you realize you are not deserving of an endless supply of unconditional love from another human. Just like your married man's wife, providing someone that endless feeding supply is impossible. This is what scared you when you got yourself out of that pool of losers. You correctly disqualified them for that very same thing, but it was much harder to see in yourself. So difficult in fact, you projected it outside of yourself onto an unpretty reality. The kind of love that is endless in its supply comes from the relationship you build with a higher power (this cannot be a human because it is impossible for them to do). It is very important that you work on this relationship because it will determine what you will be able to give to your children later. If you fail to grasp this or believe it is cruel, you will repeat this process over and over again until you grasp it and no longer think it is cruel. Everything else in between (your adult relationships) will have to be earned by you on a daily basis through your actions for the rest of your life. Your married man earned this but where he fell short was that part about not deserving an endless supply of unconditional love. He doesn't realize he can't get that from another human so he thinks the problem lies outside of him (onto his wife or a mundane reality) and this feels like a threat so he never had any guilt. Either that, or maybe feeling guilt would have required energy from him. Because his wife couldn't continually provide him with an endless feed supply, he was comforted by the idea of you securing an attachment to him. He was getting a continual investment from both you and his wife because he was too greedy to feel discomfort and felt deserving of having other people provide all of his needs so he wouldn't have to.

You engaged in that "seduction process", which felt very exciting at the time, but now it kind of feels like some foreign parasite your body just killed. This is a cycle he will continue because he never allowed himself to go through the suffering you went through to learn and to grow. You were pretty stupid about it though. Have you ever heard the phrase **"the wheel is spinning**

but the hamster's dead"? That was you and I'm glad you can laugh about it now.

Experts say that having an affair with a married man is actually perpetuating his marriage. This assertion is completely ludicrous because it's his wife that he's getting 90% of his fulfillment from, so she is keeping him in the marriage. Me saying this would have felt very threatening to you once that physical relationship was underway but now it feels like a relief. Your role is actually much less important than that because you get less than 10% and you are replaceable. This is not **personal**. For you to accept that you have a role in keeping this man married would imply that if you left him, he would be unhappy and uncomfortable and wouldn't be able to get what he needs from his wife. Had you been weak, you probably would have pulled the ultimatum card several times in response to that statement before you realized it wasn't based on reality. Please, he

57

was slightly uncomfortable maybe when he met you, but nowhere near the kind of unhappiness that would actually propel him to leave. This is a man that is so fearful of change and society wants you to believe that if you left him, he would have the courage to face his demons? So not only are you needy, desperate and pathetic but you are now responsible for his well being which means that society now designates you his higher power. The false perception our culture continues to enforce damages more than it educates. Lack of this education is why the weaker women weeded themselves out earlier on in this story. This writer's message became their identified enemy, and I simply could not contribute further to the ferocious guarding of their married man's life raft. I can't help them and I actually can't help you either because I think it's finally starting to sink in that you are your own **rescuer**.

By the way, there was no outside enemy or any inner enemy emerging within you. We just brought that fear from a less scary place to a safer one and threw out that life raft so you could be weaned slowly, calmly, and constructively. You just need to be boring for awhile although experts want you to think you have some major issues that have to be addressed before you are allowed to come back out and play.

Research shows that fear of the unknown is much more terrifying to a person than any real fear that person will accurately identify*. This is carried out predictably as a false perception we cling to because we believe that no matter how bad our situation is, the unknown is always going to be worse. It's actually the opposite. If you don't believe this occurs on a much larger societal scale, look up how much money movies like Jaws and the Exorcist grossed off of this concept. That is why they were so effective and horrifying.

The outside enemy in your case was also the unknown and it was so scary you had to project it outside of yourself onto this other person. This fear was so real and you had brainwashed yourself so well, you almost drown yourself trying to avoid it. This unknown is already here because you ended your relationship and it isn't so bad; it's actually a lot better. That married man feels pretty good most of the time too except he won't ever have the kind of full life and options you have if you continue to earn your place in this world every day like you learned earlier; you don't automatically become better than him because your out of it now. See, you weren't too far off in the beginning when you had that whole idea of him being lucky to be with someone with all these options, etc...you just got arrogant about it and expected an unconditional supply of it from him.

*In <u>psychology</u>, **psychological projection** (or *projection bias*) is a <u>defense mechanism</u> in which one attributes to others one's own unacceptable or unwanted thoughts or/and emotions. Projection reduces <u>anxiety</u> by allowing the expression of the unwanted subconscious impulses/desires without letting the ego recognize them. The theory was developed by <u>Sigmund Freud</u> and further refined by his daughter <u>Anna Freud</u>, and for this reason, it is sometimes referred to as **"Freudian Projection"**

The Memoirs

I have learned through out my 2-year affair that the hardest person to understand is yourself. I am totally heart, mind and soul in love with my married man and know that he and I belong together, but the reality is that I am 17 years to late. We have a connection that is indescribable and he has never lied to me about his marriage or home life. That puts a lot of the blame on me for the situation we have now, I should have walked away before I fell so deep. I know he loves me and he wants to be with me but the simple truth is that is probably never going to happen, which leaves me to either accept the way things are or decide that I am better than holding the number 2 spot in his life. He has 3 children and a history with her; he has a lot of hopes and dreams with me. He feels committed to stay with her and his kids and it is just time to let go for us. I don't know how to do that and I panic every time I think that time is coming close. I have separated myself from everything in my life before him, friends and options of dating. He runs the show both at home and at my house. He would never accept me going out to a bar or for sure seeing other guys, so I ask myself why I have grown to be alright with him doing it. I know for sure that I am the only girl he has ever cheated on his wife with and I know it would never happen again. He just found out how much he would have to pay for child support and alimony and since he has started to pull away from me, money is the root of all evil and it is ultimately gone to be the reason we are not together. I bought him his own cell phone on my plan so we could talk 10 times a day and we have our scheduled days of the week to be together and that works as long as I do not want, ask or expect anything more. We are there retreat form their home and marriage and they do not want to deal with any negativity when they make time to come see us. They have a whole other life outside of us, and some days it is overwhelming. Honestly, I am not even sure if I want him to leave his house for me, I just want him to want me the way he always has. The confusion and the roller coaster of emotions have totally drained me mentally and today I am asking myself what to do. I am hurt if he stays with me and I'm hurt if he leaves me.

I have been in a relationship with a married man for almost three years now and it just now came to an abrupt end. Married men never leave their wives. It is that simple. They may be miserable at home or happy with you but, it all boils down to they always stay. My advice to you is to let it go. You are going to be hurt, heartbroken and sad, but you will eventually realize how naive you were because I did. I am not trying to be mean because like I said I am in your shoes. It just gets to a point where enough is enough. There are plenty of single men in the world. You don't need to waste more years away in hopes of him one day being yours. Statistics say that less than 5 percent of married men who really divorce their wives stay with the other women. That's real talk. I am hurting now but I came to the realization in my life that I want something real and life is to short to keep chasing after a man who clearly doesn't want to be caught!!!!!!

I was involved with a married man for four years. It was a good relationship until he told his wife about the affair due to religious belief. He broke up with me because of fear to loose his family. His wife was threatening to get a divorce. I had no choice but to let him go. I am recovering but never a day I don't think of him. I hate myself because I knew from the start this relationship is too complicated. For those who are in the same situation my only advice is to get out and move on with your life. The longer you are involved the harder it gets.

This takes a lot of thinking about, an affair. My partner was with his wife for over 20 years and occasionally he even calls me the wrong name. I didn't take offence about that, but I did hate the private and sometimes angry phone calls between them that I had to tiptoe around the house during. Trying not to want to hear etc. I got cross about her divorce settlement as well, he let her have it all because he was threatened with never seeing his (grown up) kids again. Once they were really close and they still are in a way because of the shared history. She will always be family, although more of a sister, plus a very important person as mother to his kids. Things will shift and change, she will get a new partner and when she does this closeness will dilute rather a lot. I am still close to my ex husband and we all get together on our son's birthday and are friendly/polite. Not close friends but there is an unspoken understanding that we still care for each other. Wouldn't dream of being together again, no way! My ex husband's girlfriend is 15 years younger than me; an ex model. I have fought hard for even just a bit of self-belief. What I would say is that if you love him you need to try to accept him and his past, he lived another life before you were around and it has to mean something. It would be bad to make him feel that he has no right to his memories or remember good times (with his wife or without). Would you rather he said to you that he never loved his wife? I would be very worried if I though my man had been with someone all that time and pretended to love them; what would that mean about his true feelings for me? My partner's wife is more beautiful than me facially (all this beauty everywhere, how do I survive?) and I know people have said things about that to him. I, however have a much more interesting mind (2 degrees, clever me) and I have a great figure (whereas she did not). I also love him to bits and can't wait to get hold of him whenever possible. She was not really like that. My faults make me very interesting indeed! I completely and utterly adore my partner and it is that which he really wants and needs. Every time I have to meet another of his extended family I feel as though I am an exhibit and I feel very vulnerable. But I love him so much I get on with it. There is also that feeling that if he left her he could leave you (I had it). I also know she suffered enormously thanks to me. Except when you analyze it, it was not I, it was their relationship that failed. There is no reason why yours should. We all have our strengths and weaknesses, if you feel jealous say, "STOP" to yourself and re-say the reasons why he is with you that she could not fulfill and why you are special. You just have to tough it out, not act like a little girl and this time will pass. The reason you need to tough it out is so that your relationship does not get damaged by you expressing things in the wrong way and that would be the way that makes him think you don't believe in him or for that matter, yourself.

I was involved with a married man for three years. We took vacations together and saw each other every day. He told me he'd never felt as much love for anyone as he did for me. Just like practically every thing else that came out of his stupid mouth that turned out to be a big fat lie. His wife found out and he dropped me like a stone, saying he had to try to salvage something for the sake of his kids. I was stunned. He'd told me they had lived separate lives with separate beds for years. A few months later I found that everything he'd told me was untrue. His marriage was fine (or so his wife thought). They still slept together, celebrated birthdays, anniversaries. It was a struggle but I stayed well away from him and tried to rebuild my life. Now, eight months on, I'm with someone new. He is taller, younger, and sexier. And I've just heard that his wife has kicked him out. So any lady who thinks she can't live without a married man, think again. It's hard and it takes time but being alone has to be better than being with a lying, manipulative louse that only really cares about himself. And you won't be alone forever.

He was my mate, my colleague (at first), my lover, my everything, my TRUE LOVE, never met a man I felt so comfortably with, o and his humor! Couldn't imagine living without him. What a twist of faith we couldn't be together right away. I was happy to give up my marriage for him. Supposed my children would like him and his son would like me. We could cope with that. Oh, just one thing: he wouldn't hurt his wife; so kind of him. So I waited for him to sort things out. I waited four lonely years. Then I broke all contact with him. And guess what? It took me another four years to get over him and to rebuild my confidence (in myself and other people). Now I'm glad I'm broke away, but I'll warn you ladies: if you can, never go there! The pain, the agony, it is so bad and so humiliating. It'll take too much of your life.

28 years ago I met my MM. It was love at first sight. We have had the most incredible love affair ever. And I have the most broken heart. Right now I feel certain that I will die from it, but I know what wont kill me will only make me stronger. Let me explain, yes we were "soul mates". Yes, the sex was indescribably exciting. Took me to higher levels than I have ever known. Yes, we were best friends. Yes, we took trips together, spent weekends together. My heart always skipped a beat when he called. I loved

him so much. How many countless hours would I wait for him to call? How many holidays did I spend alone? How many times did I disappoint my son by making him wait till mommy got her phone call? He told me when his children graduated he would get a divorce. When that time neared, he said I have to wait until I retire because I will loose too much money. Well, that was a year and a half ago. Three Days ago I told him I couldn't go on like this anymore. I do believe that he loves me. I think he thought he would leave, but when the time came, he realized he could not hurt his children, his wife, her mother, etc. As many of you have already stated. We have to face it; these MM don't leave their wives. I don't regret loving him; I have great wonderful memories of what we had. Right now I am only sad and know that I have to work through this and move on to a different life.

We met 2 1/2 years ago but did not really go deep till about a year ago. I was pregnant with his baby about 2 years ago and had an abortion without his knowledge. Actually I tried desperately to contact him of the news but he did not answer any of my texts, emails and phone calls. I did not mention of my pregnancy but I did state in those messages that it's urgent. Well, he did not return/respond to them. So this decision was left to me even though I would be more than happy to keep the baby but financially I can't afford. After over a year...I told him in February of this year. He asked why did I not tell him before. I tried but he was in a mess with work and problems at home and I do not want to burden him with yet another which is already been taken care of. The reason it took me this long to address this to him was I felt it was the right timing and about time he knows what happened and that if he should want to leave me he can take that knowledge with him of what we have had and shared.   So he knows and then comes the part of him, wife and his kids. He made me cry at one of lunch dates when he told me he feared his wife knew about us and that he don't want to look like a monster to his kids (they are in their teens). I had told him that divorce has been since the bible times and that kids feel the tension in the family when mom and dad are having problems. Why put them thru it ... therefore we have the divorce and people divorce all the time. His answer is wife culture will not accept it and that its "losing face" if that happens. But no his wife did not find out about us it was something to do with his attitude that she was having problems. He jumped the gun. Anyway, lately he has not been talking of his wife. So during one of our meets I asked how come he don't talk of his marriage anymore. His answer was that he keeps her happy by giving her what she wants and indulging her with LV bags, jewelries ... Does that sound like a man who is going to leave his wife? My understanding is if a man wants to walk away from his wife he would not spend more than she is worth but just enough to keep peace at home definitely not expensive ruby necklace from a upscale jeweler. When his wife takes a trip he calls her constantly and checking up on her. I was there when he called her and I asked why? He says she is suppose to have lunch with her friend and he wants to find out if she is telling the truth or seeing "someone" else. Meaning her ex-lover.

I loved and still do love the married man I was with. 99.9% of MM don't leave. My old boss found out her husband was having an affair. They didn't have any children and with now having to really take a harsh look at his marriage, he decided to leave. He moved from NYC to Florida to be with the other woman. They eventually married; extremely rare. What I had to ask myself and what I pose to you is what is it that you are getting out of this and why are you allowing yourself to play second "fiddle?" For me, it was convenience, at least in the beginning. I am a single mother with a demanding job and the relationship was easy. We saw each other when we wanted to and there was no pressure. I told myself that I was having a good time and both of our needs were being met. He and I would have lengthy discussions about his marriage. I would probe him about why he stayed in a situation that he claims is so unfulfilling. Wouldn't he want something better for himself and for his wife? It didn't make sense to me. He admitted that they were incompatible and I don't think even to this day, he has ever provided a "real" answer to that question. He said a lot of it is "comfort." I had to stop asking him the questions and ask myself, what difference does it make? He's not leaving. I had to figure out how to give myself what he was giving me in a healthy way. A relationship with a married man is not healthy. He was always good at analyzing my life and everyone else's but that same analysis was always absent from his own life. I think because he was afraid of what he might see. I can't fix him and you can't fix your married man either. The withdrawal is real. There were days I felt like I couldn't get out of bed but I did. I kept going. Now a month later, I am better. I started seeing a therapist again but at least I am getting the help. He has moved on, he calls occasionally to see how am I doing and we shoot the breeze but as someone indicated we cannot be friends. The "elephant" is always in the room and no one talks about it. I had some of the best sex in my life with him. This was a man that made me comfortable with my body, my sexuality and my sensuality. We took vacations together, spoke on a daily basis, enjoyed couples massages. Hell yeah, I miss him. I'll probably always love him and I believe he loved me. He taught me a lot. When he calls, my heart still skips a beat and if he left his wife, I am sure my first instinct would be to run to him. But I am stronger than I thought. Each day gets easier. In the end, it's your decision and no one here can judge as we have all been there but from one other woman to another, love yourself more to want better for yourself. If he does leave his wife, you don't want it to be because of you. You want him to come to you as a whole person, strong in his decision and his commitment.

I too am in love, desperately in love with a married man. I have similar situations 0 stolen moments, sneaking around in cars...secret emails, secret texts. The whole bit and of course I want MORE...but he says he can not slit up with his wife for 5 more years until his children are of a certain age. His marriage is uneventful and I read above about being an enabler for him and I guess that is what I am doing. Yes I do also feel second and jealous of his wife really. He is so handsome and he really turns me on. I know it is hurting me being with him as I want more and he can't give it. Do I just be cool and get what I can get for now and wait or do I end it? I tried ending it but there is no way I can love without him. I only see him once a week and we talk everyday via email. I too am married but I m close to separating. I daydream so much of being with my married man. I know it could be awesome. I wish we could be together NOW.I wish he would break up with her so we can live our lives now together not 5 years from now. Doing this is so addictive for me so breaking up is truly hard to do as if you are anything like me you crave him and will drop everything to see him. Really by keeping busy and doing things you like to do will help out with the withdrawal. To me breaking u with my guy would mean mourning his loss and also as if experiencing withdrawal symptoms.

My relationship with my married man has ended because his wife found out and he says he has to at least try and make it work for their child. He is getting counseling and has stopped contact with me. It is breaking my heart, but my head knows that I would not want to be responsible for breaking up their family, that I would not want him to resent me if he left for me and it didn't work out, and that until he gets his own issues sorted I could never trust him. I also don't know if you can build a lasting relationship straight out of an affair and through their divorce.

I just ended a six- month affair with a MM. The last conversation we had, I asked him why he thought it was appropriate to cheat on his wife. His reaction was frightening to say the least and (thankfully) has put me off ever letting something as stupid as an affair happen again. Our conversation lead me to challenging him on the fact that again in the future, another woman would be sitting in my place, doing the same thing, feeling the same hurt. Or worse, his wife and children would find out that time and things would be 10 times worse etc. This REALLY upset him, as he hadn't been able to take the affair seriously. For him it was some sort of compartment in his life that was separate from his married one and therefore did no harm. He was so upset by my comments and straight-talking that he insisted we leave the restaurant. We shared a taxi briefly and he was silently fuming - all he could say was "so was there anything else you wanted to ask me?" I left the taxi feeling empowered and relieved. I could see him for what he really was - a coward afraid to face the pathetic life he had with his wife. He later texted me to apologize for his behaviors and to say that it was an awful experience for him. I'd held up a mirror to him and he didn't like what he saw. He said he's deluded. Deluded to say the least! Ladies, don't waste another moment of valuable time. Get out while you can and if you feel you can't, challenge your MM on the burning questions like I did. I guarantee the answers will be enough to put you off EVER doing this again. Of course, I feel sad, I feel a little lonely, hurt and deceived by him, but I would rather feel this than face more misery by deception!

I myself am in a situation like this. I start at the beginning. I met him when I was 18, just out of high school and a 3-year relationship. We hung out as friends, he was single at the time an soon we were in a serious relationship. We had a child together, got a place and were engaged. Three years later, after a very rocky relationship we split up. Not long after we were giving it another try, going to work on our problems. He met a girl, she was crazy about him, bought him things, paid for everything. When he was with her he didn't have to do anything because she didn't care. Well we never stopped, even when he was dating her we were still together. He had always told me he loved me; and we had planned to move away from here and start over. Things had their ups and downs but she never left him. She knows that he was with me the entire time he was with her but she put all blame on me an continued her relationship with him. When he got engaged and she found out about us, I put a stop to it all. I even had started dating someone, but I wasn't ready for that with someone else. I don't know if I could ever love someone the way that I love him. It was 13 months since we had been together. Well last week he was away on business and he called. I know he is miserable with the girl, but he feels stuck now because she is pregnant. Today we slept together. And I know this is wrong, but I don't know how to walk away. We have a child together so there is no way that I can do the no contact thing. I'm sure the wife knows what is happening again, he sent her an email the other day that was meant for me.

So she is begging to question him again about everything. He already has to check in with her on anything he does, I just don't know what he is doing with her. I feel like am letting myself down because I continue to let him back in after all the hurt over the last 6 years but I don't know how to let him go. There is some reason why after all the things that have gone on in the past (on both parts) that he will come back. I had even told her about us before, but he comes to me knowing that could easily happen again. If he loved her why would he risk it all just to be with me? I know he was under a lot of pressure to marry her from his family and he is not one to stand up for him self but this isn't fair! I love him and I know that he loves me, but he picked her.

I was involved with someone for nearly three years. In the beginning, he was wonderful...a dream. As time went on, he became distant and inconsistent. He always attributed his behavior to work, his "busy" schedule and jugging to balance his life, as a single, divorced dad. More and more our time and communication became limited. Our time together involved stolen moments, basically. Whenever, I tried to talk about the changes in our relationship and his behavior, he continued to blame everything on work. I wanted to believe him, but my gut knew this was not the truth. So, I began to question, if he indeed was truly divorced, contrary to being emotionally unavailable and commitment phobic. After too many episodes of crying out of utter confusion, doubt/self-doubt, loneliness, false promises and him constantly disappointing me, I decided to let it go. It was struggle, especially, when we did have contact and I foolishly allowed him back in my life. In the midst of my attempts to let to go, I tried internet dating. Well, much to my surprise, I found several internet dating profiles for him too. I was shocked by what I found on his profiles. He identified himself, in different profiles, as single, divorced and MARRIED/BORED. I was hurt, devastated and dumbfounded but it explained so much. I even found some "nude pics" of him, under some fake profiles, but I still recognized his body. This man has been doing this for a long time. I now realize this is how; he has cheated on his wife, as well. I confronted him with this but he denies his internet dating involvement. Along with that, he has not acknowledged THE LIE, about his 'MARRIAGE' not DIVORCE. I GET SO ANGRY, WHENEVER, I THINK ABOUT ALL OF THIS.... I'm angry and disappointed in him, and myself as well. After nearly a year, I have avoided relationships or dating, because of my experience with him and my past relationships. I do have trust issues with men and myself. However, I really have to rationalize this and maintain some perspective, because I do feel "my someone" does exist, regardless of my past mistakes in choosing my significant others. Also, I can't allow him or my past to have power over my life.... I have to choose to learn from my past but not live in it. I saw him, recently, after he desperately tried to get my attention. I have been avoiding him, because I couldn't deal with any of this. Fortunately, I'm stronger now but seeing him is only a reminder of his ongoing behavior, cowardice and deception. I can only rely on the fact, "The World Does Take Care of Itself"...hopefully, he will grow up and face his accountability, before the universe chooses to do otherwise. BE ENCOURAGED, LADIES.... GROW DAILY IN WISDOM & STRENGTH...

I've been with a MM for 6 years, have finally come to my senses and am in process of ending it. At the onset of our affair he wasn't yet married, only engaged. It was purely a physical relationship, however we were friends and he confided in me that both of them had serious doubts they should marry. As the date neared, and it was apparent they were going thru with it, he said our relationship would have to stop. I agreed, which was easy, as I had no real feelings for him at that point. One week after he returned from his honeymoon, he was back on my doorstep, and the affair continued. About a year and a half into our "relationship", things began to change for both of us. We fell in love. The first time he told me he was leaving his wife was FOUR years ago. May 2004. He actually left her in Nov 2004 and I was thrilled! Until, he returned to her after 6 weeks. He came back very shortly thereafter, and like a total fool, I took him back. He's left her several times since then, and he's ALWAYS GONE BACK. Each time I'm absolutely devastated, each time I take him back. I tried to justify it - life with him as a MM is better then life without him, he'll leave her one-day for good, etc. Nothing was comforting. His wife knows all about me and has for nearly 4 years, has caught him at my house many times, she and I have exchanged emails, etc and yet she stays. He's a wonderful man and as odd as it sounds even to me, I can't imagine loving anyone this way again. He says the same thing but yet, HE DOESN'T CHOOSE ME.

So here is the truth ladies - simply put, don't listen to a MM's words - only consider his ACTIONS. MM do not leave their wives. There's always a reason its "just not the right time". As in love as we are, as mediocre as he claims his marriage is, they have no children, no financial ties (she owns the house, they have no shared bank accounts, etc), her family doesn't like him, she didn't even take his last name - they're going to stick together. I read a great quote you should take to heart - I did. It was said to a woman who was contemplating, with great trepidation, ending her four-year affair with a married man - "the only thing worse then wasting four years with a married man, is wasting four years AND ONE DAY." I'm in the process of ending this relationship because I finally accepted the truth and man, is it hard. But it just became enough. I had to do it until I was done. If you find yourself in this situation there comes a point where you have to think logically and realistically. Don't delude yourself - "we're different"; "I just know he's going to leave her", etc. You gotta get your mind, life and body into another realm of existence - busy yourself with things you enjoy, force yourself to go out and socialize, pour yourself into your job, exercise, write in your journal but most importantly, keep telling yourself you did the right thing and be proud knowing you took back control of your life instead of allowing him/your relationship to control it. Sure you're gonna cry, but don't wallow in your pain - it makes it worse and does you no good. Get PROACTIVE. So if you're just starting up with a MM, END IT IMMEDIATELY and have ZERO CONTACT. You will save yourself SOOOO much unnecessary heartache by running as fast as possible in the other direction. If you're already in deep, give yourself a deadline - a personal ultimatum - of when you're going to give up and move on. And nothing ridiculous like "a year". A month or two max. And do not tell him anything about it. If the deadline comes and he hasn't left his wife, out you go and don't look back.

We ended things this morning for what seems like the 1000th time - our affair has been going on for over a year and a half. I want it to stick this time. It has to. We spent the last few nights together and finally the reality of the ridiculous situation smacked me into reality. I finally get that he will never give me and is not capable of giving me what I need and deserve. I too, never thought I would get involved with a married man. When we met and first got physical he told me he was married after the fact. He lives in a different city and like an idiot I agreed to see him again when he was in town for work. He has been cheating on his wife throughout their 20+ year marriage - he told me all about his affairs. I believe his wife knows and turns a blind eye. I justified my bad behavior - the sex was great, I had not been in a relationship for a while, work was horrible and really, where could it go - I am smarter than that. He zeroed in on my vulnerability and told me everything a woman wants to hear - my head knew it was all bs but my heart wanted to believe. Over time, of course he cheated on me as well as his wife. The last few days revealed the depth of his selfishness - or perhaps I just choose to see it really clearly for the first time. Very few friends know the depth/length of the relationship, as I was ashamed to admit I was seeing him. They would have pulled me away and knocked some sense into me. I am angry at myself for getting involved with a married man. At the same time I am sad and missing what never really was an amazing relationship. I stumbled on this sight and read every single post. I have never replied to a site before but I felt the need to thank you all for pulling me away and knocking some sense into me. The tears have stopped for now and it has kept me from contacting him today. I pray for strength to let go and forgiveness for betraying his innocent wife and kids. The stories all have a common thread - just stop it - we deserve better.

I never thought I would do something like this, but I have never loved anyone like I love him. I had the best year of my life with him. Even though he would always leave me to go home to his family, and he was only there for me when it was convenient for him. He told me he has never really been in love before me, that he needs me and can't imagine life without me. When it was too hard for me and I said I couldn't do it anymore he begged me not to throw it all away. He would talk about our future, our home, our children, and all the things we would do together. Then, two weeks ago, his wife found out. He has told me he can have no contact with me and that he needs to make it work with her for the sake of their child. He says he still loves me, and always will, but that he has made promises to his wife and he can't loose his daughter. He said he is dead inside without me, but he can't leave. He broke down when he was telling me this, and I know it was hard for him, but when it came down to it, he left me. He left me when I needed him the most. I have had to face everyone and deal with the heartbreak alone. My life is in pieces while he still has his wife, his family, and his life. I never wanted to break up a family, but I thought it was too special to throw away. He threw me away so quickly and now I am questioning everything we had. Now I'm reading this and all the stories are the same. I just can't believe everything we had was just a cliché. I am not over our break up, and it feels like I never will be. I just want to see him and see if he still cares. I need him to look me in the eye and tell me it's over to believe it. I'm just so confused. Was he really just using me? Even if it is over I need to know it was real.

I met him at work and we started dating

started working there. When I met him

was the best thing in the world. I thou

my soul mate. The only thing in my way was no

being married. We decided to go out and then things

got heated. After that we just couldn't resist seeing

each other. We tried to end it in the beginning but

that just didn't work. After that we stayed together for

year and a half. During this year and a half he told

me how much he loved me and how I was everything

he wanted in a women. We had all the same interests

and had so much in common. Every time we were

together it would feel like there was nothing else in

the world that mattered. He would make promise

after promise about us being together and having a

life with me. Just recently he told me that he was

leaving his wife and that he promised that we would

be together and he wouldn't leave me. Well just a day

after that he then decided that maybe he should work

it out and leave me and not be with me. I am so heart

broken over this. I have been talking to my best

nd, which really doesn't help because she really doesn't know how it feels. I have really just come to the conclusion that if he needs space then that's what I have to give him. I keep saying to myself that if its meant to be than it will be. I just need to move on as quickly as possible and leave this all behind me. Its not easy losing someone that you love to someone else.

I ended our relationship after 2 years because finally it had become more painful to stay than I believe it will be to live without him. The balance had shifted and I spent more time miserable than happy. I was only happy when were together and spent the rest of the time second-guessing what was happening in their relationship. I spent countless hours and days analyzing everything he said to me, reading between the lines trying to discover his truth as he always would tell me he was confused, he loved his wife like a sister and now he had found true love, compatibility, fun, honesty etc with me and he didn't know what to do. He wanted children someday and I had already had mine and unable to have any more so a life with me would mean no kids and that added to his confusion OR was this just another excuse for not being with me. I feel gutted sad and lonely today and I miss him desperately as we were worked together and were friends for 9 years attracted to each other and started a more personal friendship 5 years ago and then commenced our intimate bonded relationship 2 years ago. He moved away 6 months ago and we talked on the phone several times a day and many text messages, I have seen him about 8 times since he moved, and it has all done my head in and my heart is broken BUT I have peace in my mind that I have done the right thing and I no longer feel like I am approaching emotional melt down, Yes I am sad but I feel in control.

All I know Girls is:

Don't spend another minute helping him live out a 100% happy life.

You are making it possible for him to stay in an unfulfilled marriage.

Make him accountable.

If he can fall for you someone else will too.

Take back control and discover what his true intentions are.

Believe in yourself.

The meaning of stupidity is to repeat the same behavior and expect a different outcome.

Don't be tempted to txt or call him it will only reaffirm to him that you can't live without him!

After two years, I now realize that he never really did love me, appreciate me, or seriously consider a future with me. I was just his temporary escape. And, when he decided that he didn't need me anymore, he discarded me like yesterday's newspaper. Before, he complained about how his wife treated him, and how he felt obligated to stay in the marriage for the kid, but now he is saying that he has always wanted to be with her and insists that we "move on and put this behind us." So easy for him to say because it has always been about him, when I foolishly believed he really wanted me. I can't even tell you to what extent I stupidly bent over backwards to give him so much because I fell for him so deeply, even when I consistently got so little or nothing from him. The immeasurable pain, emptiness, feeling of worthlessness, unbearable loss, anger, feelings of rejection.... all make it something to avoid like the plague. The pain is just horrible, horrible. I feel dead inside.

I was in a relationship for 10 years with a married man who happened to be a church pastor. It was STUPID of me to believe the "tragic story of his marriage" and how he must serve God first place before the eyes of people... but he is able to tolerate adultery as a side dish. OF COURSE he claims he loves me and OF COURSE he made me believe we are soul mates. How I fell in love with him is a something I'll regret but after years of struggle I LEFT HIM 7 MONTHS AGO. I feel GREAT, he sends messages I don't answer, I blocked his emails, I don't answer his phone calls, and I HAVE disappeared from his life. I have to add, we had some form of sex but for some reason maybe guilt or whatever we never competently had sex. I've never had another man and although I have been blind of love for him for years, at last I feel strong. LET THE MARRIED MAN GO ON WITH HIS IMAGE, boost your self esteem, AND BELIEVE that God SEES EVERYTHING. Consequences we will have to pain with pain, emptiness, loss... but this will last a while, repentance and obedience guarantees you'll get through, and in the End he will give us all what we ask for. A person that's real, with whom to share our lives and be happy and have the home we all dream of. Dreams can only come true, if we follow the right path and let go of the lies. Even a very good man has a selfish heart. We don't have to be part of their fantasy... when we CAN AND WILL have a life of our own. And believe me, It will be better than the one he has... cause ours will be based on truth and maturity that comes from getting up after the fall. People who don't accept their faults, just go on reproducing them all over again and getting hurt and hurting all. I don't want those consequences... mine as they are... are enough. Hold on tight! Leave him. Do the right thing to do... and you will harvest the fruit of a good seed. We have to die to our will and our flesh, to be reborn into a better person, humbler and with a clean future. The blood of Christ can heal all wounds, if you let him. God Bless You.

I have been seeing a married man for almost a year now it started out as just sex and now I can not imagine my life without him he is kind and compassionate and some times all we do is just sit and snuggle. We often talk of had we meet years ago before we were married. I can honestly say I love him and I know that he loves me. The problem is he is trying for a baby with his wife. This breaks my heart and I always say tonight will be the last night I see him but I can never bring myself to leave him. I too am married my husband works nights and is never home, when he is he is always sleeping and just doesn't give me the attention that I want and need. I wish I could leave them both and find someone like my lover who is single. My lover is the perfect man he cooks he cleans and he is the best lover I could have imagined. None of my friends would understand so I have kept this all to myself. I just needed someone to talk to about it

I to am in love with a married man. We have been seeing each other for the past 2 1/2 yrs. I met him at a cook off in big "H" (he's in a well known band in SA) and it was instant attraction for both of us. He is 38 and I am 40. He has been married for 18yrs and has 3 kids. He has never said one bad thing about his wife. He does love her, but they apparently have lost that spark or zing that was once between them. For the first year he would come see me almost every other month because his second job would allow it. Once he was laid off and got another job, then it was me going to see him, maybe 4 times a year. This past year I probably saw him 5 times. We talk everyday by cell and email and he tells me how much he loves me. He has introduced me to many of his friends and the band has even been to my house when they played in big "H". Sometimes I feel as though he doesn't really care if he gets caught. Just on New Year's in SA, I was with him as he played at a club and some of the band's wives "figured" me out. Then he doesn't go home as usual, spends the night with me at a hotel and uses some excuse of to tired to drive home or he's been drinking to much and needs to stay at work and sleep there. I would never buy that one being that I too, have been on the other side. He has expressed how he wished he had met me back when we were in our early 20's. We get along so well, conversation especially and yes of course sex, but that part is just the bonus as we both see it. I believe we both will keep seeing each other till whatever happens. We have a strong bond between us and we really understand each other. If something were to happen, we would be together. But I am not forcing him and nor do I want it to be that way. I think he does want to divorce, but it's his kids that he worries about and I do understand that. I never had any children, but

I grew up with parents who never divorced, so I can only imagine what it would be like without. I can only say that he is the love of my life and it has me feeling great even with our distance. It's a chance I am willing to take. We all have to make our own choices in life and be willing to live with what the consequences will be.

I'm coping with a break up from a married man right this very day! He broke up with me this morning over the phone while I was at work. I'm also married. However, this affair had been going on for about 4 years, and for some odd reason, I have always felt and still do after the break up, that this person is my soul mate. I feel hurt right now, a little empty, trying to figure out how not to call him or send him text messages. But yet I figure, this time next week, I will be okay. If I can get through just one week of not talking to or seeing him, I'll be fine. When he told me that he was tired of lying to his wife, and being committed to her will make his life so much easier, I couldn't do anything but respect that! I appreciate his honesty, but for some odd reason, my gut is telling me that he's gonna reappear sometime in the near future, only to be the same person he was before. He shared a lot with me about issues in his marriage, and I think this was him really trying to give it one last try because they do have children and a lot invested in one another. I would often ask myself why am I doing this to my husband. I mean, my husband is a great man, a wonderful father, excellent provider for his family, down to earth, good-looking, hardworking, and intelligent. He cooks, cleans, fixes everything, always tries to make sure I have everything I need and want to make me happy, and allows me to be my complete self! My ex-affair partner would always say that I had too much freedom to be a married woman, and that he would never allow his wife to do the things I was able to do. But now let me tell you this, my husband has been suspect of affairs on many occasions. Don't know if this is the real reason why I indulged in an affair, but I truly believe that he gave me all the freedom for him to gain the freedom to be able to do what he wants to do. It's like a revolving door, the cycle just continues on. What keeps me going through all of this? My spirituality, my strength, and my stability! My friend broke up with me and I'm accepting that, don't regret anything about the relationship. However, when he comes back, and believe me, he will, I hope I can be strong enough and have a clear head in telling him that I cannot indulge in this kinda relationship again, and walk away with my dignity!

I ended up in an affair with a man who is based in the same office as me - probably purely for the excitement etc, etc, but having said all that I fell in love with him. Again, he told me from the outset there was no happy ever after - as he put it - so he immediately covered his back. I have now told him that I don't want to see him anymore - this relationship was one-way and destroying me emotionally. It really hurt to do this but I know for my sake it is absolutely for the best. All I am going to say is this - be honest with yourselves. These men don't love you; if they did truly love you they would leave their wives. The only road these relationships lead to is your unhappiness. You deserve better. Go out and find a single, doting, caring partner who genuinely loves you and would do anything for you - they are out there!

I have been dating a married man for almost three years now. We are both married and have children, and to make it even harder, we don't even live in the same country! Neither one of us had ever cheated before. We both said we never would. We met online and thought the distance of 3000 miles should be safe. After a year of talking online or on the phone almost every day, for hours and hours, we decided to meet only once. I had a business trip to his country and he made up a reason to be in the same city at the same time. It was only supposed to be to meet face to face and have a drink. To make a long story short, we fell hopelessly in love and after a wonderful weekend together, it was time for me to go back home. After that we spent even more time online and on the phone, visited each other almost every month and the love only got deeper. A couple of months ago I told him I had asked my husband for a divorce. That decision had nothing to do with him, but since then, he's been distant. I have tried to convince him that I will never ask him to leave his family for me but I have the feeling he doesn't believe me. This man has made me happier than I have ever been, I have never loved anyone so much and I have never felt so much love. He still tells me he loves me, talks about our next meeting but I sense something is different. I refuse to let him hurt me and I have been telling myself for weeks that I should break it off, before he does. The problem is, the minute he's online or on the phone, it's like nothing happened and it's not until after he's gone that I tell myself, "I should have ended it". I despise people who cheat on their spouses. I thought that was something I could never do but here I am. What hurts me the most is people who judge "us" without knowing the whole story. People cheat for different reasons. I can't agree with those of you who say your married man should leave his wife, even if they have children. I admire a man who puts his children first. I would never leave my children for a man and I would never expect a man to leave his children for me. In my dreams, my married man leaves his wife... we are both single and free to do whatever we want. Yet, I never see myself living with him. Isn't that strange?

Unfortunately it is very hard to control your feelings, when it comes to love but I also believe that if a married man loves another woman, not his wife, he will feel responsible for her life and feelings. If from my side it is not a selfish love from his side it is very much selfish. I don't think this kind of man deserves that kind of selfless love. If you ask a bit more for yourself, you will see how much selfish he is, he will be scared to loose a reputation, will ask you not to tell anyone who asks you about him that you do not know him, he tells you that he did not give you any hope for more than free love and that he was with you because you needed it more. I agree with those who think that we, women, should respect ourselves more and do not love those who just use our love as selfish people.

He was the love of my life. We got together in high school and I had a child that I aborted my senior year. We lost touch and ran into each other 2 years ago. We both were married but I was actually separated while he was still w/his wife. The one he of course told that he didn't want to be married anymore and therefore lived his life as if he were single. They had a seven-year age difference where he was the younger one and they didn't have much in common. He would constantly tell me how unattracted he was to her. He gave me is business card the night we met and I hesitated to call him. About the third week I broke and called him because I honestly could not stop thinking about him. Looking back I realized I made the biggest mistake of my life. It's been two years and he has left his wife and had we were together for the most part. He stayed with his mom but I had full access to him I enjoyed it until he changes job and runs into a woman that he cheated with before me and finds out that they have a 3 year old baby girl that she didn't tell him about because she didn't want to cause any trouble. He's still not divorced but separated and now he has the mother of his child who he never mentioned after him to complete her family. I am so sick of all the time I wasted with him. I have some good memories and at this point have chosen to walk away and let him dig out his own mess. I will love him forever but I realize he is damaged goods and regardless of how comfortable I am with him we would never have a healthy relationship. I fell as though it is my punishment for knowingly dating a married man something I never have done or will do again.

I met my married man online; we met in person and are planning to meet again. The only time we speak is on Instant Messenger or the phone (I had to buy him a calling card so his calls to me wouldn't show up on his bills). After reading so many of your posts, I think I CANNOT BE IN LOVE WITH HIM; it's more like an addiction. His wife once gave me what may be the best advice we can all take when she said, "Be careful what you wish for, you may just get it." I think we should head that advice and start to treasure ourselves more...in some deep part of ourselves, we KNOW we have more self worth than this!!! Don't misunderstand me, I have great empathy for all of you and for myself...what I need more of is a sense of self worth, self esteem, and yes, self love.... when I learn to love myself the way I deserve, I won't allow myself to settle for the demeaning way all "other women" are treated. If we are honest with ourselves, the married men who say they love us, only demean us by asking us to accept anything less than first place in their lives. Loving on the sidelines and settling for crumbs is not the Miriam-Webster definition of love. I say let us discover our authentic selves and let us be strong enough to stand alone...without the emotional and mental abuse that loving a married man brings us. After suffering from severe depression, losing my job, alienating my friends and family for a married man....

I have been in love with a married man for years. We once carried on an affair for almost two years and since have had encounters. He was my one and he got away over 14 years ago and married another woman. I have never met her and never want to either. See him and me have a history before her, he has never had children of his own, has adopted her two though, we lost one when we was together. Before he got married to her he tried to find me through a friend but the friend told him I was already married (which at the time was not true) since I have been in couple disastrous relationships and he has always been there. This man I know was and is my soul mate.

We try to not do this but it is like once we lay eyes on one another it is there. I know he has no intentions on leaving his wife now nor have I asked him to...I guess we were meant for another lifetime but no matter if he is married, he is with me or her, or we have or do not have an affair this man is the world and he will always will be to me. He is the one that makes my stomach drop and my heart bounce and my soul ache. He is the one but just not mine. It is such a heartache to love someone you will never have...but then we do not get to choose who we love...life sometimes does not go with what we feel but instead by what we have to do...He has obligations and he would not be the man I love if he did not honor his obligations. So I will be with him in the next life..until then I will love him from afar. Or sometimes closer but I will always love him...true love is something that always does not come along...I would have rather loved him then to not have loved at all...I will always wish him and his family the best because it is true...even if we can't help how we feel...so what I am getting at is being in love with a married man is not your fault because if it is love it is not something you can control...but wanting him to leave obligations he has made is not love either...it is selfishness and everyone including me is somewhat selfish to have these affairs...but maybe one day we will get forgiveness.

I too fell in love with a married man and our affair just ended. I really love this man and I thought he loved me. But now I've come to realize that if he REALLY loved me he would never have put me last and stayed married. Even with children. It just doesn't work that way. When you love someone and you are really each other's soul mate, nothing else matters. You have to be with that person to make everything else right in your life. He wasn't willing to do this, and so I've slowly and painfully come to realize he wanted it all on his terms; for me to make him happy, her and their daughters to keep the perfect picture going. What he loves isn't me, isn't his daughters, isn't his wife, isn't the perfect picture. He loves HIMSELF, above all else! God, this hurts. I never thought I would ever do anything like this, but here I am.

I have no one to talk to about this matter and am in so much pain that I am going literally insane. I feel so helpless and alone in this. If someone could please comment or provide advice, I would be most appreciative. For the past year, I have been involved with a married man. Before the involvement, we were very close friends, would confide in each other about things and he would vent about frustrations he would have about his wife. Then, we became honest about how we felt with each other and then started a relationship. He was everything that I had hoped for in a man--he was sensitive, listened to me, said things that made me feel loved, appreciated and understood, like no one else in my life. Then, 6 months into the relationship, he said that he thought we should break off the relationship because he made the decision to stick with his wife and child. He said he was resigned to sticking with her for the sake of the child. I remember being so heartbroken. Ever since then, we would have peaks and valleys. He would me that we should just be friends and that he can't continue the relationship, but then he would still be intimate with me. So, his words were not consistent with his actions. I just couldn't let go of him and it seemed like he had difficulty letting go of me too. All the while, it was very painful knowing that he was going home to someone else and sleeping with someone else. Every night, I would think about this. I started to think that his relationship with his wife probably wasn't that bad. He would use his child as an excuse to stay in the relationship, but I started to wonder whether he still loved his wife more than me. Even with all these agonizing thoughts, I was so in love with him, that I would still long for the next time I'd see him. He now has told me that he definitely, absolutely cannot have this relationship with me and wants to just be friends. He says that he loves me, but I don't believe him. My mind is so messed up. It seemed like he loved me, but now, it seems like his feelings towards me have suddenly changed and he doesn't care if he ever sees me again or not. The indifference and lack of emotion in his voice is so crushing. He told me that about a month ago, he planned a trip with his wife that they will take next month. It makes me think that all along, he loved his wife more than me and things were never really that bad between them. The jealousy and anger that I feel is consuming me to the point that I cannot function. I feel so incredibly used and abandoned. The emptiness is unbearable as for so long, he was the only thing that occupied my thoughts and brought me happiness, excitement, etc. I can't stop thinking about him. Deep down inside, I had believed that he would ultimately choose me. He kept holding on to me and I kept hoping. Now, he has discarded me. I don't understand how his feelings changed so quickly. How can I stop thinking about him and obsessing?

I love him more than anyone; he's married with a little boy. I can't sleep; I have that empty pit in the bottom of my stomach. We became best friends in a year. Nothing but honest friends with the special bond of everything we liked and had in common. After one year, we kissed, after that kiss, the kissing went on for a month, and then we actually slept together. It was so incredible, makes me believe that I never slept with anyone I actually loved before. Now I'm afraid that this is a once in a lifetime relationship, I will never emotionally or physically feel like this again. I am 38 and know better. I know the statistics say he will never leave her. But I believe that he truly loves me. I am not strong enough to let him go. I even tried the religion thing, prayed for God to let me find someone that is available and not to want what isn't mine, hasn't worked. To my credit though, I will say that

I have not taken myself off the market. I go out probably every other weekend and seriously look for someone to date. No one catches my eye. You just fall in love and you can't help it. That is why you can't stop it. So I guess I will pray that God let's me fall in love with someone else.

Soul mates, I couldn't believe it when I met him. We are each other's sidekicks. He is married, has two wonderful kids, and a beautiful wife. After a month, I went to his house, stayed there, met his wife, and met his kids. They knew nothing about the fact that I was having such a remarkable relationship with him. The kids fell in love with me. His wife had no idea. It was the weirdest most uncomfortable situation I had been in. Watching the interaction with his wife, trying not to feel jealous. After all it is his WIFE. I grew to love him, so very much, love his kids, and love his wife...(as much as I wanted to be her) why did I continue with this relationship! We shared our dreams, future, and the uncertainty about the whole thing. We saw each other as much as possible. I am not one to condone cheating. He knows that. It's so hard. I kept praying for strength to end it. He doesn't want to hurt his kids. That's understandable! Then why am I being so selfish? I was selfish cause I thought I could make it work...long run...you can't.

I have been in love with a MM for 14 years. I left my first husband because I loved this man so very much. At first he couldn't leave because his kids needed him, he was the 'provider' and it was his 'duty' to provide. I have 4 kids of my own, his are now all grown up with kids of their own. Now he can't leave because he has done the 'kid' thing, so we are waiting until my kids are grown up and having lives of their own. Perhaps he'll come to my funeral, because I'm not getting any younger. He's in his early 50's now, me late 40's and I love him more than words can say, and I agonize every day of why I am in this situation. Even if after 14yrs I can't tell my friends as we live in the same town and I know his wife. There will be many people who think badly of me, but his wife only looks upon him as a provider, there is no love or affection - but I still envy her the 'connection' she has with him.

I, myself, am in love 1.5 years now with a MM. I am 25 yrs and he is 40 yrs old. The unusual thing is that because of the nature of our job, we spent last year more or less 6 months together in different countries without having to share him with his family. I almost forgot that he was married. He would almost never reply to his wife's calls, when he was with me and did not talk about her. However, every time we would come back to our country, I had to face the reality. He promised that he would get divorced this summer, but of course you know what happened. He still keeps saying that he will get divorced at some point, just does not specify which year this will be…! The usual excuses! What I wonder though now is, if I really want to be with a man like that?! He tells me that his wife will divorce him at some point and maybe it is true. He spends a lot of time with me, too many phone calls, sms etc. They also have 2 kids, the youngest one is 1,5 years old... It drove me crazy when I found out! He started seeing me when his wife just had his baby! Firstly I didn't know, but even when he told me, I was already so in love with him that I didn't leave him. I cried a lot, but I stayed and that's what I regret! All these MM (married men) have been living double lives for x years. Time period full of lies and acting! Can you really trust a man who can do that? Have you wondered what he will do to you, if you become his next wife? Today he does it to her, why not tomorrow to you?! This is what I ask myself everyday. I am still in love with him. He is the only man I said that I would like to have family with, but I decided that I will try to fight it! Such a man cannot be trusted, and I know that in the future, he would make me unhappy. It is crazy that even though I know it, I have not moved on yet. I feel like I am addicted to him and I hate myself for that! I want to get the power to say, "the end"! I am not sure if

I will manage to do this soon, but one thing I am sure about: We all deserve something better! Not to be living in the "shadow" of their wives!!!

I was involved with a married man for three years. We took vacations together and saw each other every day. He told me he'd never felt as much love for anyone as he did for me. Just like practically every thing else that came out of his stupid mouth that turned out to be a big fat lie. His wife found out and he dropped me like a stone, saying he had to try to salvage something for the sake of his kids. I was stunned. He'd told me they had lived separate lives with separate beds for years. A few months later I found that everything he'd told me was untrue. His marriage was fine (or so his wife thought). They still slept together, celebrated birthdays, anniversaries. It was a struggle but I stayed well away from him and tried to rebuild my life. Now - eight months on, I'm with someone new: taller, younger, and sexier. And I've just heard that his wife has kicked him out. So any lady who thinks she can't live without a married man, think again. It's hard and it takes time but being alone has to be better than being with a lying, manipulative louse who only really cares about himself. And you won't be alone forever.

My situation is a little different in the way that he was very manipulative to keep me where he wanted me. He never told me he would not leave his wife, in fact he told me dates he was going to file & lied about seeing attorneys. The dates were always pushed to future dates, but it left me with the hope. Looking back, I realized he didn't love me; he just lusted after me. If he loved me and if he loved you, he would never make you suffer through the agony and the pain that this type of relationship will bring about. He would never allow it to drag on and on. I think if any of these relationships work out, it's because he leaves within a certain period of time. If it's been a year and he had not left, the chances are he is never going to leave. Let's face it, at that point why should he? He has the passion and excitement with us " when they want us " and the security of his wife to go back to. I had to ask myself this very painful question, I've wasted two long years believing in his lies and hopes for our future, do I really want to waste one more moment of my life? The pain may hurt when you leave & I understand how hard it is to take that step. But trust me when I tell you that if you stay the pain will become far worse, because deep inside you have to know " you deserve so much better " and what you are now doing is putting your life on hold so a man who cannot commit to you or his wife can enjoy himself temporarily are your expense. I was devastated when I ended it and it took so much time to heal. But the happiness and the joy I feel today is far greater than any of the pain he caused. Try to focus on what life has in store for you; what person may be right around the corner for you. You will never find the right man when you are holding on to the wrong one.

*"It's fear of the unknown. The unknown is what it is. And to be frightened of it is what sends everybody scurrying around chasing dreams, illusions, wars, peace, love, hate, all that--it's all illusion. Unknown is what it is. Accept that it's unknown and it's plain sailing. Everything is unknown--then you're ahead of the game. That's what it is. Right?"

~ John Lennon

Rules for Dating a Married Man:

Don't call him after hours. Get used to talking to him from 8-5 and only when he wants to talk to YOU.   Also, let him phone when he wants to so there are no obligations and false expectations on your part; you lose your sense of dignity when you are constantly disappointed that he doesn't call when he says he will.

Never talk bad about his wife or listen to his complaints about her. Look at your watch if he starts talking about how irritating she is or how she doesn't listen to him. There's nothing more degrading about being his therapist when your time with him is limited. Ask him about his day and listen to him talk about HIMSELF.

Don't complain about what you are not getting from him. This is like pouring cold water on a flame. He is with you so he can be free of relationship expectations so keep it light and fun. He gets this nagging from his wife already.

Always dress well and keep your toenails painted; make the special effort. He is with you because you offer some excitement and sexual stimulation outside his marriage and he will be comparing you to her.

Don't explain your daily whereabouts to him. You are not his property and he gets his 'time off' when he's with his family.

Don't assume you are the only one he's seeing. Many married men juggle one or more mistresses at a time. Also don't assume you are the first affair he's had so don't ask. You don't command his exclusivity.

Don't let domestic responsibilities intrude. This is a sure fire way to kill his infatuation with you. Other than baths and showers together, keep other bathroom activities behind closed doors.

Don't try to be a domestic goddess by cooking 4 course meals for him. The last thing you want to be is his 'wife' or 'mother'. He already gets this at home and you'll just remind him of what he's trying to escape. You are there to be indulged, not used, so keep him on his toes and keep your activities out of your house.

Stay confident. If you want to be treated special, you are going to have to stay on top of your game and act special. This means taking care of YOU and staying a 'prize'. No unshaved legs, think garter belts and perfumed lotions….

Let him know upfront that if he falls in love and leaves his wife, you'll leave him.
Set boundaries and ground rules. Make sure these protect you and your reputation.

Don't panic if he says he loves you. Don't believe him either. This is a man who tells his wife he loves her when he's with you. This isn't the kind of love you can count on.

When you become emotionally involved, he WILL hurt you. This is about fun and excitement, not about pain.

Assume his marriage is stable. Most men who have affairs are not looking for an exit. If he is, you don't want to be the next wife he's unfaithful to.

CPSIA information can be obtained
at www.ICGtesting.com
Printed in the USA
LVHW082236250121
677502LV00041B/1026

9 781440 450044